Laurence King Publishing
www.laurenceking.com
ISBN: 978-1-78067-969-3
Printed in China